BETTER BLURB WRITING FOR AUTHORS

OLIVIA ATWATER

STARWATCH
PRESS

Copyright © 2021 by Olivia Atwater
https://oliviaatwater.com
All rights reserved.

No part of this book may be reproduced in any form or by any electronic or mechanical means, including information storage and retrieval systems, without written permission from the author, except for the use of brief quotations in a book review.

INTRODUCTION

I used to *hate* writing blurbs. As an author, it only makes sense that I prefer long-form writing—*why*, I used to wonder, was I expected to sum up thousands of words in the space of hundreds? But I've always been an analytical sort, and eventually, the lure of learning a new skill was too much to pass up. I finally got frustrated enough with my blurb-writing that I decided to fix it.

I don't remember much of the week that followed. I ingested just about every resource I could find on blurb-writing, free or otherwise. I read blurbs from other bestselling books in my genre and tried to figure out what made them work. I drafted and redrafted my existing blurbs until I was frankly sick of looking at them.

My next book was shockingly successful. And I was absolutely certain that it was because I'd agonised over the blurb until it was perfect.

Since that time, I've found myself in a position to help other authors polish their blurbs. I like helping out other people, and even when I'm very busy, it only takes me an instant to drop a few notes in chat that could make a blurb incrementally better than it was before. But it's finally occurred to me that I keep repeating the same advice over and over, such that I really ought to just write it down.

What follows is all of the same advice I would normally offer to an author who says "hey, can you take a look at my blurb?" It includes the process I use to write my own blurbs, along with a few tips about searching for genre-specific blurb conventions. I've included real examples from my own blurbs, in order to illustrate each of these steps, and I've also included a few examples of other blurbs that I've worked on at the end. These examples mostly fall within fantasy and its subgenres, because I speak the most with other fantasy authors—but the advice should be generally applicable to any sort of genre fiction.

I'm sure that there are other methods out there for blurb-writing; but this one hasn't failed me yet, so I'll probably continue using and refining it for quite some time. I hope it's useful for you, as well.

CHAPTER 1
OVERVIEW

This book starts with an overview of **How Readers Select Books**, and some brief notes on **When to Write Your Blurb** and **What Goes in a Blurb**, before moving on to my personal blurb-writing process.

I start the blurb-writing process by writing up a **One-Click List**, where I parse out all of the most interesting and/or marketable aspects of my book and rank them by how important I think they are to my readers. Then, I write up a **Lead Line** which includes all of the most important aspects at the top of my list. I start the actual text of my blurb with a **Tempting Hook**, and move on to some **Plot Development** before landing upon a **Question**. Lastly, I write a **Sales Paragraph** which explicitly states the genre and the atmosphere, and I do a few editing passes of **Tightening Words**.

After I go over the blurb-writing process, I'll offer a few addendums about **Genre-Specific Blurbs** and give some tips for **Editing Blurbs** rather than writing them from scratch. Lastly, I'll give several other **Example Blurbs** which I helped to edit, along with explanations about the editing choices. (All authors were asked for permission in advance to include both their original blurbs and the reworked versions.) At the very end of the book is a short **Evergreen Blurb Template** to remind you what goes where.

CHAPTER 2
HOW READERS SELECT BOOKS

WHAT READERS WANT.

I know you're probably eager to get onto the blurb writing process—but don't skip ahead! The following section goes into some important details that could require changes to other parts of your marketing process.

Generally speaking, a prospective reader who is actively searching for a book will go through the following process. A reader might stop at any point in this process, and either put the book back or decide to buy it without further investigation.

1. **Narrow their search by genre.**
2. **Search for titles and book covers of interest to them.**
3. **Select a book that piques their interest and read the blurb.**
4. **Read a sample of the book.**

Your goal as an author is to make sure that readers who are looking for a book like yours not only see it, but also accurately identify it as something they would truly enjoy reading. Ideally, your cover should be so on-point that readers who *wouldn't* enjoy your book never even click on it—but your blurb should also work to weed out readers who would dislike your book. In short, you are aiming to write a blurb that is both accurate and compelling to the *right* readers.

This is why it's so important to know which genre your book belongs in. When readers describe the sorts of books they enjoy, I have never once heard a reader say "I would like a truly unique book that doesn't fall neatly into any particular genre." And yet, so many authors *describe* their books in that way, as though it's a selling point!

Genres are not a bad thing; they are a filter system for readers who know what they like and who would prefer not to waste their time reading something that they already know they don't enjoy. If your book doesn't fall neatly into any particular genre, you are going to have great difficulty recommending it to a reader before they tune out and go searching for something they *know* they're going to like.

If you're not sure which genre your book falls into, go looking at retail websites or at your local bookstore, and check what's on the shelves. Look up books that you consider similar to yours, and see which genres they're categorised in. Above all else, however, avoid the squidgy "this book is unique and cannot be categorised" trap.

Once you have your genre nailed down, look at other covers in your genre and make sure that yours fits in with them. It's important that your **cover** advertises your book accurately, as readers use covers to guess at what the book might contain. You might have the most beautiful cover in the world—but if it uses cover elements which are generally associated with young adult novels, and your book is actually a hard-boiled detective story, you're going to have a lot of excited people clicking on your cover and then navigating away in disappointment.

Once you're certain that your cover accurately conveys what a reader will most enjoy about your book, *then and only then* will you be able to sell your book effectively to prospective readers with your **blurb**. Understand that when a reader first picks your book off the shelf or clicks on a thumbnail of the cover, they have seen something in that cover that interests them. As soon as that reader starts scanning the blurb, they are looking for *confirmation* that what they believed they saw in the cover is actually in the book itself. If your expensive, eye-catching cover and your beautifully-written blurb do not match, then all of your efforts will be for naught.

Your blurb should also demonstrate the actual style of your writing in some way. It's not enough to claim that your book is a thrilling adventure; you must actually *make* your blurb thrilling. If you've written a comedic book, then you should have at least one well-crafted joke in your blurb. A reader who perceives a mismatch between the blurb itself and what it claims about the book it describes might well put the book down.

Some readers will go a step further and **read the first few pages** of your book, in order to confirm that they enjoy your writing style. Because of this, it's often a good idea to give extra editing attention to the first few chapters of your book—and especially the very first line of your book. Writing a compelling story obviously falls outside the scope of this guide, but it can be helpful to understand that a beautiful cover and blurb might still fail to engage readers if your first few chapters are not immediately exciting enough.

Now that we've discussed how readers go about selecting a book, what conclusions can we take away from the process?

1. **Your book requires a genre.**
2. **Your book's genre must be accurate.**
3. **Your book's cover must fit the genre.**
4. **Your book's blurb must confirm as soon as possible those things which the reader believed they saw in the cover.**
5. **Your blurb must prove any adjectives it claims about the book it describes.**
6. **Your book's first line and its first few chapters should be particularly engaging.**

This guide can help you write a good blurb in general—but a well-written blurb will still fail if it does not match your genre or your cover.

CHAPTER 3
WHEN TO WRITE YOUR BLURB

BLURB BEFORE YOU WRITE.

Most authors don't think to write their blurb until after they've finished the novel—but the longer I've been an author, the more I've come to realise that having your blurb done *before* you write can be extremely valuable. Because a blurb highlights the most exciting, most marketable aspects of your book, it can be a great tool during the writing process. A finished blurb can serve to remind you what you've promised your readers and what they'll be expecting in the book once they open it.

These days, I actually tend to write my blurbs after I've finished my outline but before I've written the book. Once I write the blurb, I sometimes go back and revise my outline in order to align it more closely with the blurb. Then, and only then, do I actually settle in to write the novel.

In the worst case, you might finish a blurb, and then discover during the writing process that the book is *nothing* like your blurb. Obviously, if your book runs off the rails like this, you can always revise your blurb again.

CHAPTER 4
WHAT GOES IN A BLURB

WHAT A BLURB SHOULD HAVE.

"Describe the sort of book that you enjoy reading."

No really, give it a try now. Make a list of all the things you *love* in the books that you read.

Most people will list things like: **genre** (fantasy, romance, murder mystery, heist, thriller), **time period** (Regency, Victorian, Medieval, contemporary), **age range** (Middle-grade, Young Adult, New Adult), **level of sexuality** (clean, low heat, high heat), **level of violence** (PG, dark, grimdark), **tropes** (chosen one, road trip, fake marriage, enemies-to-lovers), and **similar books** ("if you enjoyed *The Lord of the Rings*, then you'll enjoy this one"). Like my younger self, they might add something along the lines of: "Is there a dragon on the cover? I want a book with dragons. And no space ships, please. Just the dragons."

These descriptors are how people choose the book they want to read next. Generally speaking, the **genre** is the most important aspect—it narrows the pool significantly, and it implies a lot of these other aspects, which is why book retailers group their shelves by genre. But once a reader walks over to the fantasy shelves, they're probably scanning the book covers and blurbs to make sure they don't accidentally read a grimdark fantasy when what they're really after is a romantic fantasy.

This, therefore, is the main purpose of your blurb. When a reader is looking for your book and doesn't know it yet, you want them to read the blurb and be immediately reassured that they're in the right place. Conversely, if your book is *not* what the reader is looking for, your blurb should make that clear as well.

WHAT A BLURB SHOULD NOT HAVE.

Notice what wasn't anywhere on the list above?

That's right. Your plot.

Readers do not want a point-by-point summary of your story from your blurb. They want to know which *parts* of your plot are of interest to them, without having the whole thing spelled out for them. Younger me didn't care how a book began, as long as I knew that it was eventually going to have a dragon. I checked the cover for dragons—and then I checked the blurb to make sure that space ships were not going to sneak in and ruin my dragon fun.

It's absolutely crucial that you excise this misunderstanding from your brain while writing your blurb. You don't need to tell the reader everything that happens. You don't even need to clarify details which could be read in more than one way, as long as they're irrelevant to the parts your readers most care about. Sure, you *could* spend an extra paragraph explaining why your main character has Special Powers because she has a specific kind of fire magic that's rare within your magic system—but really, all your reader wants to know is that your main character is unique, and she makes things go boom.

HOW YOUR BLURB IS LIKE A MOVIE TRAILER.

I often tell other authors that their blurbs are a movie trailer, and not a movie synopsis. If your book was a horror movie, your readers wouldn't be interested in an exhaustive explanation of the main character and their history, and they definitely don't need to know the first victim's name. All they're really looking for is a creepy, atmospheric shot of the haunted house, a brief voice-over line like "the locals say it's haunted," and a sudden glimpse of a woman they don't know being stabbed in the back. Maybe there's a brief shot of some bloody words on a mirror: "no one leaves alive." All of these things give the reader a great idea of whether they'll enjoy this particular movie or not... and none of them require an in-depth explanation.

If I were to write that movie trailer in a more blurb-like format, it would probably look something like the following:

The house on the hill is haunted… and no one is making it out alive.

At first, Ella is thrilled to inherit an old mansion from her uncle… but soon, she starts hearing whispers that a ghost still wanders the house. By the time Ella invites her old friends over for a party, she's already starting to think she ought to burn the place down.

When the first person turns up cut to ribbons in the bathtub, Ella *knows* she should have torched the house and left for good. But it's far too late: the bloody words on the mirror say that no one's getting out alive.

CHAPTER 5

EXAMPLE: HALF A SOUL

In the following sections, I'll describe the process I use to write a blurb. This includes making a **one-click list**; writing a **lead line**; starting paragraph one with a **tempting hook**; writing a **plot development** into paragraph two and ending it on a **question**; and wrapping up with a **sales paragraph**.

As I walk you through this process, I'll be using my blurb for *Half a Soul* as an example. I've printed the full blurb below, however, so that you have an idea of what we're going to end up with.

It's difficult to find a husband in Regency England when you're a young lady with only half a soul.

Ever since a faerie cursed her, Theodora Ettings has had no sense of fear, embarrassment, or even happiness—a condition which makes her sadly prone to accidental scandal. Dora's only goal for the London Season this year is to stay quiet and avoid upsetting her cousin's chances at a husband... but when the Lord Sorcier of England learns of her condition, she finds herself drawn ever more deeply into the tumultuous concerns of magicians and faeries.

Lord Elias Wilder is handsome, strange, and utterly uncouth—but gossip says that he regularly performs three impossible things before breakfast, and he is willing to help Dora restore her missing half. If Dora's reputation can survive both her ongoing curse and her sudden connection with the least-liked man in all of high society, then she may yet reclaim her normal place in the world... but the longer Dora spends with Elias Wilder, the more she begins to suspect that one may indeed fall in love, even with only half a soul.

Pride and Prejudice meets *Howl's Moving Castle* in this enthralling historical fantasy romance, where the only thing more meddlesome than faeries is a marriage-minded mama. Pick up *Half a Soul*, and be stolen away into debut author Olivia Atwater's charming, magical version of Regency England!

CHAPTER 6

THE ONE-CLICK LIST

WHAT MAKES A READER ONE-CLICK?

Now that you have a general understanding of what we do and do not value in this process, it's time to make a list of desirable traits from *your* book. Keep each item in this list down to short, understandable phrases; if you can't summarise the idea in four words or less, then it's probably not common enough for readers to be actively searching for it in a blurb. If you're editing an existing blurb, you can actually look through your existing reviews for comparisons to other authors and for the things your readers loved the most; for more detail on this, read the later section on **Editing Blurbs**.

Once you've finished your list, you'll want to reorder it, prioritising those items which readers feel most strongly about and which the largest number of readers will find interesting. Your genre should almost always end up near the top of this list, since so many readers find it to be an important filter. The top few terms on your list should be things which make a reader one-click buy.

EXAMPLE: HALF A SOUL.

Half a Soul currently has my most successful blurb to-date—as I would hope, since it's the book that most of my readers pick up first. When I was originally making a one-click list for it, here are the items which popped out.

- Regency-era
- Romance
- Fantasy
- Faeries
- Magicians
- Grumpy love interest
- Whimsical tone
- Compare to: *Pride and Prejudice*
- Compare to: *Howl's Moving Castle*
- Satire

I would consider this list to be roughly in the correct order. Here are a few reasons why.

Regency-era.

Historical readers often have a favourite era which they'll always buy, and little interest in any other era—a Regency reader wants to know immediately that this book is of interest, so it's important to put the Regency era at the top of the list. "Regency" is also a genre all on its own, which implies several things already: it means that the book will probably have balls, romance, social conflict, and marriage proposals. This one word does an awful lot of work to reassure the reader that they are exactly where they wanted to be.

Romance.

This book centres around a romance, though it doesn't skimp on the fantasy plot. Many romance readers are genre-specific and will not entertain a book without a romance, so it's important to put this near the top. Some readers *despise* romance and will not touch it, and it's also important to me that those readers do *not* buy this book. Accurate advertising leads to happy readers.

Fantasy.

Fantasy readers are not quite as picky as romance readers—they are more likely to read a book with any sort of magic, regardless of its secondary genre—but they still want to know that there is going to be magic of *some* kind before they commit to a book. Thus, fantasy goes high on the list, but slightly below romance.

Faeries and Magicians.

Both romance and fantasy readers often particularly enjoy books which contain certain supernatural creatures. Younger me wanted dragons, and I considered it very important to see a dragon on the cover and in the blurb. Somewhere out there is a reader who wants faeries and a reader who wants magicians. If I'm lucky, they might even be the same person.

Grumpy love interest.

This book isn't quite enemies-to-lovers, but the male love interest *is* quite grumpy. This is important for more reasons than one, as I mention later under **Genre-Specific Blurbs**; it's important to describe both romantic leads in a romance blurb, as the interesting part about a romance is how those two characters fall in love.

Whimsical tone.

This book has a whimsical tone, akin to a real faerie tale. It's incredibly PG, and safe for very picky mothers to give to their young adults. The book is *not* grimdark fantasy, and it is unlikely to satisfy readers of that genre.

Other book comparisons.

This book was inspired at least in part by both *Pride and Prejudice* and *Howl's Moving Castle*, and it compares favourably in tone to both. I tend to put direct comparisons to other books at the bottom of a blurb, however, as I want people to be interested in the book for its own sake, and *then* to be reassured about its tone and atmosphere through these comparisons.

Satire.

This book is definitely satire, and the satire is one of my personal favourite parts about it. But generally speaking, people would not walk to a "satire" shelf in the bookstore and expect to see my book there. Anyone specifically interested in satire is probably seeking literary fiction and not genre fiction; meanwhile, my genre fiction readers don't *mind* the satire, but they probably aren't specifically seeking it. Because of this, satire goes at the very bottom of my list—and in fact, it ended up dropped from the blurb entirely.

CHAPTER 7

THE LEAD LINE

THE TOP 3.

I start every blurb with a bolded lead line at the top which encapsulates the top 2-3 items on my one-click list. Writing a good lead line is both an art and a science; you want to work in those one-click items so that the reader is reassured that they are in the right place, but you *also* want to create enough intrigue that most of your readers will continue on through the rest of the blurb.

To be clear, your lead line can *strongly imply* the items on your list, without being literal about them. You don't need to call your book a fantasy if your lead line says "Ella is a wizard on the run." Wizards only happen in fantasy novels, and even the most distracted reader isn't going to mistake your book for anything else when you've handed them a wizard in the first sentence. The exception to this rule is a book's specific historical time period, if it isn't contemporary; because Regency novels mostly take place within London society, you can't simply say "Napoleon has just been defeated" and expect your readers to understand that this means it's a Regency novel. As such, it's generally just best to put the word "Regency" (or whichever time period you've written) into the lead line as-is.

Above all else, you should make sure that your lead line *clearly* conveys your genre. If your lead line is so generic that it could fall into several genres, you're going to lose a lot of prospective readers. For instance, I have often seen lead lines like:

She's running for her life. He's running from his past. But maybe they can save each other.

This lead line tells me nothing about the genre, and even less about the characters and the plot. It could just as easily describe a fantasy novel (a wizard on the run from an evil cult meets an assassin trying to forget their past), a contemporary thriller (a key witness in a murder case flees the killer and runs into an ex-government agent), a paranormal romance (a mortal woman who stumbles into a supernatural curse requires protection from an angsty vampire), and so on. You can easily see how a reader who enjoys any one of these scenarios might find the other ones deeply off-putting. Eliminate any potential uncertainty, and make sure that you've made your genre clear in your lead line.

A BIT OF INTRIGUE.

Like the very first line in a novel, your lead line should be short, pithy, and instantly intriguing. If you're struggling to figure out how to accomplish that, here are a few tried-and-true techniques you can use.

- **Establish a theme.** Some books have a very clear central theme, or a question that the reader is meant to answer by the end. Example: "Ella knows that home isn't always where the heart is."
- **Establish the main character's problem.** If your main character has a really interesting problem, you might want to lead with that. Example: "When Ella clicked her magic slippers, she expected them to take her home. Instead, she's found herself in a terrifying new world, full of nightmarish creatures."
- **Establish a tone or a character's personality trait.** If your main character is quirky, or if they have a very strong tone, you can sometimes hook readers on learning more about them. Example: "Ella's always known that she could take over the world… if only she could make herself get out of bed before noon."
- **Set up an apparent contradiction, or a shocking statement.** An interesting statement that doesn't make immediate sense will convince most readers to keep going in order to get the explanation. Example: "Ella is pretty sure she's

slated to die next week—and frankly, she's looking forward to it."

- **Set up a dangling question.** Similar to the apparent contradiction, you can write a lead line that omits at least one key detail and therefore keeps people reading. Example: "Ella is officially, legally dead—but at least no one can say she died because she was stupid."
- **Establish an important character relationship.** If your character has a central relationship that defines the story or their personality (for instance, parental relationships in a young adult novel, or a budding attraction in a romance), you can centre this relationship in the lead line. Example: "After Ella burned down her treehouse for the second time, her father said he wouldn't teach her any more magic."
- **Describe one of your main character's strongest opinions.** If your character has a strong opinion, you can open by stating it as a fact and going on to describe why they hold that opinion. Example: "Boys with wands are dumb. That's what Ella tells herself every time the male-only Sorcerer's Guild rejects her application, anyway."
- **Express the character's values.** Similar to a strong opinion, you can start with a value that the main character holds dear. Example: "Family is everything. Even and especially after they're dead."
- **Set up a unique skill.** Is your character the

absolute best at something? The reader probably wants to know about it! Example: "Ella can talk her way out of trouble in every language on earth."
- **Set up a crucial plot point.** Maybe your plot really hits the ground running, and you want to make sure the reader knows it by hitting them with a major plot point. Example: "Ella has been running for her life, ever since she stole the Key of Doom."

You can probably already see how some of these lead lines accomplish several goals at once. You should always be thinking of ways to save space while conveying several things as elegantly as possible.

THE FOLLOW-THROUGH.

Whatever you decide on for your lead line, you *must* remember to follow through on it in the rest of your blurb. Return to your lead line often while you're writing your blurb, and ask yourself whether the rest of that blurb answers any questions, implied or otherwise, which you presented with your lead line.

EXAMPLE: HALF A SOUL.

You might remember that the top 3 items on the one-click list for *Half a Soul* were:

- Regency-era
- Romance
- Fantasy

Here is the lead line for the book, which incorporates all three items:

It's difficult to find a husband in Regency England when you're a young lady with only half a soul.

You'll notice that I've explicitly called out the historical era with the word *Regency*. I've also implied romance (there will be husband hunting) and fantasy (the main character has only half a soul). I've also set up plenty of questions to be answered in the rest of the blurb, such as: how did this young lady end up with only half a soul? What does having half a soul do to a person, and why does it make husband hunting more difficult?

As we go on, you'll see that I make sure to answer the questions I've posed in the lead line. But this lead line is already 50% of my battle; it's the line that most people will see, especially when I advertise the book with a service that has limited space for ad copy.

CHAPTER 8

THE TEMPTING HOOK

START AT THE RELEVANT PART.

The first paragraph of your blurb—the hook paragraph—should start at the beginning of the most interesting part of your story. Many authors mistake "the beginning" for the beginning of the main character's life, but this is a poor way to begin a blurb. Compare the following two opening lines:

> *Ella grew up in the suburbs with a white-picket fence and two dogs.*
>
> *Ella died last night, and she can't remember how it happened.*

Unless the white-picket fence is absolutely crucial to the story, the reader is way more interested in starting from the second sentence. Omit the fence. Omit the dogs. Go straight for the jugular.

You'll often find in practice that you try to start from the most interesting part of the story—and then later discover an even *more* interesting part of the story from which to start. This is a normal part of the blurb editing process; in fact, I've sometimes written an outline, then written the blurb, and discovered during blurb-writing that the *book itself* should start from a different point in the story.

WHAT GOES IN THE HOOK PARAGRAPH.

Now that we've got an opening, it's time to make sure that our hook paragraph includes the following:

- Further development of the one-click list items from the lead line.
- Some progression towards answering any questions we presented with the lead line.
- A few more items from the one-click list, if possible.
- An introduction to your main character, and something interesting and/or compelling about them.
- A pleasing, logical flow from one sentence to the next.
- An intriguing end to the paragraph, so that the reader feels invested in continuing the blurb.

This is *all* that you need in your hook paragraph. You don't need to include every single plot and subplot. You don't need to mention every character in the book. Stay brief, punchy, disciplined, and on-topic. Resist the urge to stray into things which aren't either one-clickable or else *absolutely necessary* to the logic of your blurb.

Remember our movie trailer analogy, from **What Goes in a Blurb**. Your blurb should convey an atmosphere, a few exciting images, and some important tropes. If you're not sure which parts of your book belong in the blurb, consider queuing up some movie trailer music and daydreaming up a trailer of your own book. What voice-over lines were important enough to go in there? How did the scenes build in tension? What was the very last thing you saw before the words **Coming in October 2021** flashed on-screen?

Write that trailer into a blurb. Don't choke your readers with details; instead, lightly whet their appetites.

EXAMPLE: HALF A SOUL.

The first paragraph of the blurb for *Half a Soul* is as follows:

> Ever since a faerie cursed her, Theodora Ettings has had no sense of fear, embarrassment, or even happiness—a condition which makes her sadly prone to accidental scandal. Dora's only goal for the London Season this year is to stay quiet and avoid upsetting her cousin's chances at a husband... but when the Lord Sorcier of England learns of her

condition, she finds herself drawn ever more deeply into the tumultuous concerns of magicians and faeries.

You may recall that *Half a Soul*'s one-click list included the following:

- Regency-era
- Romance
- Fantasy
- Faeries
- Magicians
- Grumpy love interest
- Whimsical tone
- Compare to: *Pride and Prejudice*
- Compare to: *Howl's Moving Castle*
- Satire

The paragraph above elaborates on the Regency era aspect ("London Season"), introduces a potential love interest ("The Lord Sorcier"), establishes some of the fantasy elements of the setting (faeries and the Lord Sorcier), and explicitly mentions both faeries and magicians.

The logical flow *also* elaborates on the questions introduced by the lead line: Theodora Ettings lost half of her soul to a faerie, and the practical effect of this is that her emotions are muted. The reason this makes it difficult for Theodora to find a husband is because she's prone to accidental scandal.

This paragraph ends on a line that implies danger: Theodora is about to be drawn into a plot to do with magicians and faeries. Hopefully, the reader wants to keep going and hear more.

CHAPTER 9

THE PLOT DEVELOPMENT

RAISING THE STAKES.

The second paragraph in your blurb should continue the tension you've started up in your first paragraph, and raise the stakes or develop the central plot thread in some intriguing way. This can take a few different forms, depending on your plot. It could be:

- **An extra complication ("this bad problem has now been made worse").**
- **A sudden twist ("this problem isn't what it initially seemed to be").**
- **A character introduction ("someone else also has an interest in this problem").**
- **A secondary problem which must be solved at the same time as the first one ("not only is X a problem, but Y is also a problem").**

As you might have guessed, you should also be using your second paragraph to work in any one-click elements you couldn't manage to fit into your first paragraph. You may not fit *all* of your one-click items into your blurb, and that's all right—it's why I always make sure to prioritise my list before I get to writing the blurb, so that nothing truly crucial ends up being omitted.

Depending on the genre, the second paragraph might trend towards introducing either a potential romantic partner or the villain/foil to the main character. In a romance blurb, it is always expected that introducing another character with their own paragraph implies that character to be the other half of the romance plot—and this bias can creep into other blurbs, if the genre feels murky. Thus, if your book dabbles in a romantic subplot, you should be very careful about introducing a villain in the second paragraph, as readers may interpret this character to be an edgy love interest!

EXAMPLE: HALF A SOUL.

The second paragraph of *Half a Soul*'s blurb is below.

> Lord Elias Wilder is handsome, strange, and utterly uncouth—but gossip says that he regularly performs three impossible things before breakfast, and he is willing to help Dora restore her missing half. If Dora's reputation can survive both her ongoing curse and her sudden connection with the least-liked man in all of high society, then she may yet reclaim her

normal place in the world... but the longer Dora spends with Elias Wilder, the more she begins to suspect that one may indeed fall in love, even with only half a soul.

Because this is a fantasy romance, I have introduced the love interest more fully in the second paragraph. I've dedicated at least part of that paragraph to describing that he is a **grumpy love interest**—which was one of my remaining one-click items. In this case, Elias is both a plot development and a complicating factor in the problem which I presented in the lead line; because he has a poor reputation, and Theodora is forced to associate with him, Elias is likely to make her husband-hunting prospects even worse. Of course, any halfway-savvy romance reader will realise that at this point that Theodora is likely to fall in love with *him*.

CHAPTER 10

THE QUESTION

ASKING THE QUESTION.

The development section of your blurb needs to leave the reader with a question of some sort—the kind of question that can only be answered by reading the book itself. This does not mean that you, the author, have to *ask* a question; you can instead suggest an uncertainty, and allow your reader to ask the question for you.

Some of the most common questions you'll find include:

- **Will the main character manage to save the city/the country/the world?**
- **Will the main character fall in love with the obvious love interest?**
- **Will the main character satisfy their revenge?**
- **Will the main character escape a pressing danger?**

- **Will the main character save someone they love?**

Obviously, the reader often knows the answer to these questions already—for instance, romance readers know that the answer to "will these two people find true love" is always going to be "yes." But bringing up the question tells the reader that *this* will be the focus of your book's plot. If the reader likes your question, then they'll probably pick up the book.

EXAMPLE: HALF A SOUL.

You've already seen the question in the blurb for *Half a Soul*. In fact, I've sneaked in several questions—none of which *look* like explicit questions.

> If Dora's reputation can survive both her ongoing curse and her sudden connection with the least-liked man in all of high society, then she may yet reclaim her normal place in the world... but the longer Dora spends with Elias Wilder, the more she begins to suspect that one may indeed fall in love, even with only half a soul.

Will Theodora's reputation survive her curse and her new association with the grumpy Lord Sorcier? Will she reclaim her normal place in the world? Can someone with only half a soul still fall in love? All of these are questions to which the reader requires an answer, and any one of them might be the question that makes them decide that they simply must read more.

CHAPTER 11

THE SALES PARAGRAPH

TELL, DON'T SHOW.

We've finally reached the end of the narrative blurb! But there's one more thing left. You've just spent a few paragraphs implying the one-click aspects of your book—now, it's time to state them outright, so that the reader is absolutely certain that they're in the right place. I sometimes call this the "tell, don't show" paragraph.

In this paragraph, you especially want to include:

- **Genre.**
- **Comparison books.**
- **Whether the book is part of a series.**
- **The title of the book.**
- **The author of the book.**
- **A direct call to action ("pick up *title*", "buy *title* now", etc).**

You *can* get a little fancy or flowery with this paragraph, but you absolutely have to work in the above information.

The direct call to action should be your very last sentence. Ideally, your reader got so engrossed in your blurb that they might have forgotten they were even reading a blurb; they're now excited about your book, and you want to remind them that there is indeed a buy button attached to this blurb, and that they can buy their own copy of this story if they click that button.

EXAMPLE: HALF A SOUL.

Below is the sales paragraph for *Half a Soul*.

> *Pride and Prejudice* meets *Howl's Moving Castle* in this enthralling historical fantasy romance, where the only thing more meddlesome than faeries is a marriage-minded mama. Pick up *Half a Soul*, and be stolen away into debut author Olivia Atwater's charming, magical version of Regency England!

You'll notice that I've included my comparisons right off the bat. These comparisons don't have to go first, but they certainly can—and I've had enough *readers* sell my book to other readers with the comparisons above that I know the comparisons are both on-target and very important to whether someone thinks they'll like the book or not.

Firstly, notice that I've repeated that this book takes place in Regency-era England, since "Regency" is basically a sub-genre unto itself. But I've also used the genre "historical fantasy romance", which is really a combination of two genres ("historical fantasy" and "romance"). I wouldn't normally recommend doing this, except that this book really does fall squarely in the middle of the two genres; it has full plotlines that fit into both genres, and generally speaking, a reader of either genre will find what they're looking for in the novel. Most of the time, you want to be sure you've identified a single, exact genre; for instance, urban fantasy is *very* different from paranormal romance, and if you market your urban fantasy with a romantic subplot as "paranormal romance", your paranormal romance readers may end up rightfully miffed at your long digressions into non-romantic plot.

The stylistic choices ("marriage-minded mama", "stolen away") and the adjectives I've chosen ("charming", "magical") are both things I've used to reinforce the whimsical atmosphere (one of my one-click items). In this case, I've done a *little bit* of showing, as well as telling—but most of my showing still happens primarily in the earlier narrative blurb. I've still been as blunt as possible in this last paragraph about what the reader will find in my book.

CHAPTER 12

TIGHTENING WORDS

MAKE IT SHORTER. NO, EVEN SHORTER.

Sometimes, I'll do several drafts of a blurb before I find one with which I'm mostly happy. At this point, I turn my attention to editing the blurb. My main goals during this stage are:

- **Use fewer, more evocative words.**
- **Prune any unnecessary synopsis-style information that's made it into the blurb.**
- **Make sure each sentence flows logically into the next sentence.**

A prospective reader's attention span is limited, and every spare word is another chance to lose that attention. Once your blurb starts hitting more than three short paragraphs, you start to run the risk that a reader will simply tune out and click away. This is especially problematic if you're trying to market your book as a page-turner; if you *say* your book is "a wild, action-packed ride" but your blurb is seven paragraphs of rambling setting information, your reader isn't going to believe that you're *capable* of writing a wild, action-packed ride.

Check through each sentence of your blurb in turn, and ask yourself whether the reader absolutely *requires* this information in order to understand the one-click elements. If the answer to that is yes, then ask yourself whether there's a much shorter way to say the same thing. Below are some examples of easy wins.

- Search for adverbs like "very", "extremely", and so on. Replace these adverbs and their follow-up adjectives with something shorter and punchier. Example: "very happy" could be replaced with "ecstatic".
- Search for possessive word chains and reword them to make them shorter. Example: "the magical key that Ella owns" could be replaced with "Ella's magical key."
- Remove entire statements and replace them with an adjective that modifies a character. Example: "As Ella struggles to save the world, she finds herself missing home" could become "Ella is homesick and struggling to save the world."
- Drop overly-long explanations of setting-specific details; instead, use more generic terms, or else make sure that the surrounding context makes it clear to the reader what you're talking about. Example: "Ella discovers that she is a pyroclast, a

rare type of sorcerer who can use fire magic" could be replaced with "Ella discovers that she possesses a rare and frightening fire magic."

Lastly, of course, you need to make sure that your blurb **makes sense** as-written. A lot of authors will read their blurb out loud in order to force their brain to engage with it in a new way, and I highly recommend this. In particular, I've noticed that a lot of authors will edit up their blurbs to stuff in all of the information they require... and then accidentally end up with strange clauses that make no sense. For example:

> "Ella needs John's help if she's going to survive the night. But Ella is also starting to fall in love with him."

At first glance, these two sentences *look* as though they belong together. But once you read them aloud, you might realise that the *but* makes no sense without further context. As-written, these two sentences imply that John might stop helping Ella if she falls in love with him, which doesn't track. It's possible that there's more context that could explain the missing logic here, but the reader won't intuit that logic unless you give it to them. As such, a potential fix might look like this.

> "Ella needs John's help if she's going to survive the night. But Ella is also starting to fall in love with him—and she promised herself that she would never fall in love again."

As you practice your blurb writing and editing, you'll get better and better at spotting these problems. But it's always worth a last look to make sure that you haven't accidentally mangled something during the editing process.

CHAPTER 13

GENRE-SPECIFIC BLURBS

BUT THE BLURBS FOR OTHER BOOKS IN MY GENRE DON'T LOOK LIKE THIS AT ALL!

Not all blurbs will follow the pattern described in this guide; some genres tend towards first-person point-of-view blurbs, for instance, or somewhat more stream-of-consciousness blurbs. Romance blurbs almost always dedicate the first paragraph to the main character and the second paragraph to their love interest. Some genres will have books that start with their book comparisons in bold, such as: **Readers of X author will love this new release, set in Regency England.**

Given that I cannot possibly be an expert in blurbs of all genres, I will not attempt to explain each genre here—especially since genre conventions can also change over time, and any genre-specific advice I offered might well end up outdated. But there is a process to figuring out what the blurbs in your genre look like; it mostly involves looking up the best-selling examples at any given moment and searching for the commonalities between them.

You should always check what the blurbs in your genre look like—but it's also important to add a caveat here that not all successful books are successful *because* of their blurb. An author who happens to be a whiz at online ads might successfully promote their book in spite of a confusing or lacklustre blurb, especially if their ad copy and images are so fantastically on-point that readers have already decided to buy the book by the time they reach the blurb. That same author might discover that their book would sell even better if they tightened up their blurb; as such, you should always use hard sales data to decide whether one blurb is performing more successfully than another.

Much of the advice in this guide will improve your blurb no matter the genre, even if you have to tweak certain aspects of it to match the current fads. Importantly, the advice in this guide will *always* give you an "evergreen" blurb, which you won't have to adapt in order to suit those changing fads; the template in this guide is generic enough that most readers won't blink to see it in any genre. At the end of the day, I would recommend that you aim to strike a good balance between "well-crafted blurb" and "blurb that looks similar to other blurbs in your genre"—but I'm afraid I can't describe what that balance might look like for you in particular.

CHAPTER 14
EDITING BLURBS

EDITING AN EXISTING BLURB.

You can use the process outlined in this guide to edit up an existing blurb. I often go back to my old blurbs and give them another editing pass, to see if I can continue to improve them. If you do edit up an existing blurb, however, there are some extra tips to keep in mind.

- **Read your reviews before you write your one-click list.** If your book has already been out for a while, you should go through your online reviews and check which keywords your existing readers use to describe your book. Maybe you thought your book was a paranormal romance, but your readers have unanimously decided that it's actually an urban fantasy. Romance readers are also particularly good at picking out tropes in their reviews, and you can always count on them to offer up enthusiastic adjectives that describe the book's main love interest.

- **Benchmark your sales before you change your blurb.** Readers are a tricky bunch, and they don't always like the things that authors expect they will; as such, it's always best to get a solid sense for how your book is performing before you make any changes to your marketing. Once you've got a good benchmark for how your book performs in an average week, change just one thing about it—your cover, your blurb, or your first few pages—and then let your book sit for another full week of sales before you change anything else. That way, if your new blurb is a miss, you'll have some hints on how to continue editing it; and if you continue iterating on your blurb, you'll always know whether you're headed in the right direction or not. (One caveat: if your cover *and* your blurb are both off-genre, you'll need to change them both at the same time, in order to avoid losing readers over an obvious mismatch.)

CHAPTER 15

EXAMPLE BLURBS

Most authors reading this guide probably already have blurbs they'd like to polish. As such, I've asked a few authors for permission to include blurbs I've worked on with them. Each section here includes **the original blurb**, a **one-click list**, a **new blurb**, and an **explanation of edits**.

By the time you read this guide, some of these books might have changed their blurbs again—and that's okay! As I mentioned in the section on **Editing Blurbs**, it's good marketing practice to try different things and see how well they work. Iteration is a good thing, and you can't know what will actually work until you've given it a test run.

CHAPTER 16

EXAMPLE BLURB: WESTERN GOTHIC FANTASY

The following blurb describes the Western gothic fantasy *Blood Bounty*, by Liza Street.

ORIGINAL BLURB

Three things annoy the hell out of Gracie Boswell: noisy saloons, handsy cowboys, and vampires.

Ever since a bloodsucker took down her pa, Gracie's sole mission is the extinction of the vampire species. She travels the west on the dime of sleepy little towns who are more than happy to toss her a coin for the trouble of clearing their trouble. But she's not the only bounty hunter on the job, nor the only one with a score to settle.

To rid the west of otherworldly outlaws, she'll have to trust someone to watch her back. What choice does she have when failure means ending up in a shallow grave?

Featuring a badass heroine who isn't afraid of slinging charms to fight evil, *Blood Bounty* is a fast-paced adventure for lovers of urban fantasy and weird west tales. Get your copy and ride through the magical desert prairie today!

ONE-CLICK LIST

- Historical fantasy/western gothic (genre)
- Vampires
- Mages (charmslingers)
- Outlaws
- Reluctant buddy cops/posse
- Dark atmosphere
- Fae
- *USA Today* best-selling author

NEW BLURB

Gracie Boswell's got a charmed bullet, a brand new posse, and a pack of outlaw vampires to kill.

The tiny town of Penance has a big vampire problem—and charmslinger Gracie Boswell aims to be the solution. A whole nest of vampires makes for a mighty fine bounty, though, and Gracie is far from the only charmslinger angling for the job. When a charming local layabout and an old competitor elbow their way into Gracie's posse, she's forced to at least pretend to play nice...but trust is scarce in the west, and smart bounty hunters always sleep with one eye open.

But Gracie doesn't have much time to watch her fellow bounty hunters—Penance's vampire nest is bigger and more organized than anyone suspected, and there's at least one traitor in the town's midst. Soon, Gracie finds herself in the unenviable position of leaning on her posse...and at least one of them isn't what he claims to be.

***USA Today* best-selling author Liza Street continues to thrill with a brand new western gothic series of outlaw vampires, sinister fae, and good old-fashioned treachery. Pick up *Blood Bounty* for a wild ride through the dark and dangerous west!**

EXPLANATION OF EDITS

I enjoyed my advance copy of *Blood Bounty* so much that I offered to help Liza edit up its blurb—I felt like the original blurb just didn't do the book justice, and I wanted more people to read it!

Blood Bounty is a dark Western gothic novel with a lot of witty attitude—but Liza also writes paranormal romance, and her branding on the cover originally looked a lot more upbeat than the book really was, with a smiling gunslinger and a lot of bright colours. This book was *not* a paranormal romance—it was dark and bloody, with only a tiny romantic subplot, and it was full of vampire-killing. The new cover, centred on a winking skull, used a Western font and more muted colours. We therefore rewrote *Blood Bounty*'s blurb to match that cover.

The new lead line conveys all of the most important one-click elements on the list above: the novel clearly centres around vampires in a Western setting, and it further mentions charms (magic). It uses the words "posse" and "outlaws", which add an obvious Western flavour that accurately represents the tone of the book.

The first paragraph characterises the main character, Gracie, and sets up the dark, paranoid atmosphere of the book by centring around the deadly vampire problem and Gracie's suspicion of her fellow bounty hunters. It also conveys the buddy cop trope—or in this case, the "buddy posse" trope, as three of the characters are forced to work together despite their differences.

The second paragraph throws some interesting wrenches into the plot and raises the stakes—and then, it confirms that Gracie's paranoia is justified. The subtle question at the end of the second paragraph is: which character isn't what they appear to be? What sort of trouble will this cause, given how tense the rest of the situation already is?

The sales paragraph mentions one of Liza's most important credentials as an author (one of her books hit the *USA Today* bestseller list, so she can refer to herself as a *USA Today* bestselling author). The sales paragraph also explicitly states the genre, and it backs up that genre with plenty of appropriate adjectives ("sinister", "wild ride", "dark and dangerous west"). We also added in a brief mention of the fae in Liza's setting, as they feature more prominently in later books in the series —but because the fae only appear in one scene in this first book, we limited their presence to the sales paragraph.

Overall, this new blurb conveys the dark atmosphere a bit better, and it squeezes more of the most important information into the lead line. Crucially, it also mentions Liza's bestselling credentials, which can often mean the difference for a reader on the fence.

CHAPTER 17

EXAMPLE BLURB: PARANORMAL ROMANCE

The following blurb describes atmospheric paranormal romance *Leviathan's Song*, by Elsie Winters.

ORIGINAL BLURB

With the magical mafia knocking down the front door, the last thing Elara needs is to follow the seductive song calling her outside her shop...

Elara is well versed in creating beautiful things with the potential for great destruction, and the moment she meets Levi she knows that's exactly what he is. Charmed and irritated by the seductive siren, Elara is drawn to him, but though his siren song pulls her in, his words push her away.

As a landlocked half-merman, rejected by his people, Levi is used to wanting things he can never have, and the soft-hearted and strong-willed Elara just hit the top of that list. She's tempting, and that's dangerous for him.

He should stay away.

But when an underwater city's distant war comes to Elara's doorstep, she's suddenly in over her head, and Levi can no longer bear to keep his distance. Can she trust the mercurial siren that calls to her with more than his voice?

LEVIATHAN'S SONG is a slow-burn paranormal romance about a girl caught between multiple magical factions and the mysterious merman she longs for.

ONE-CLICK LIST

- Paranormal romance (genre)
- Merman
- Tragic, brooding love interest
- Bonded mates
- Bodyguard
- Magical voice
- Rich/poor romance
- Part action, part political intrigue
- Elf

- Lead with a unique/special power
- Mage/magical crafter
- Comparison: Ilona Andrews
- Comparison: KF Breene

NEW BLURB

As Elara races to save a dying city, her best hope lies with a seductive siren... but brooding Levi has his own reasons for keeping her at arm's length.

As an elven weapon smith, Elara is an expert in crafting beautiful, deadly things. When an underwater city known as the Deep sends for her help, she's determined to answer the call... but between murderous gangsters and razor-sharp foreign politics, Elara is ill-equipped to handle the situation on her own.

Levi Navarre is half-merman and all brooding, sardonic wit. Landlocked, jaded, and rejected by his people, the last thing Levi wants to do is get involved in underwater affairs. But soft-hearted, strong-willed Elara is a temptation he just can't resist... even if she *is* several miles out of his league. Levi has good reason to avoid the obvious magical bond forming between him and Elara—but if he isn't careful, then playing bodyguard could soon turn into something more...

> Readers of Ilona Andrews and KF Breene will enjoy debut author Elsie Winters and her atmospheric paranormal romance, full of love and magic. Dive into *Leviathan's Song*, and succumb to a magical temptation...

EXPLANATION OF EDITS

The first thing I talked about to Elsie was actually the cover for *Leviathan's Song*. It was a gorgeous, artistic cover with an elf in a fantastic-looking dress. As such, I assumed that her novel was a fantasy romance and not a paranormal romance—but Elsie soon clarified that the novel starts in Seattle and takes place in a modern fantasy setting. As such, while the readers who *did* buy her book enjoyed it, many of them mentioned that they had been expecting a more medieval story than the one that they got.

Elsie has since gone to work adding the male lead to the cover (hopefully in more modern clothing), in order to convey the more contemporary setting. As such, we'll assume that the new cover conveys that the novel is a paranormal romance, and therefore attracts readers of paranormal romance to read the blurb.

After sorting out the cover/genre mismatch, we brainstormed all of the potential one-click elements in *Leviathan's Song* and made a list, as above. The original lead line had some pithy bits (I personally love the idea of a magical mafia, and I have a weakness for alliteration), but ultimately, some of these things didn't have enough prominence in the story to justify putting them in the lead line. We therefore spent most of our time trying to come up with a new lead line that would immediately convey the genre and suggest a few of the specific romantic tropes in the story.

The new lead line covers a lot of ground at once (magic, romance, a merman, and a brooding love interest). As such, we can give a little more room in the first paragraph to Elara, the female main character. This allows us to follow a specific genre convention for romance blurbs, wherein each paragraph is dedicated to one of the two romantic leads.

Since this book had already been out for a while, we were able to read through reviews and pull out certain keywords to describe the male romantic lead, Levi. Some readers called him sarcastic, aloof, brooding, etc—so we did a little bit of work with a thesaurus and made a comprehensive list of similar words we could use in his paragraph.

Lastly, we retooled Elsie's sales paragraph, using adjectives and comparison authors that her readers had suggested. We ended this sales paragraph on a clear call to action. This new blurb conveys more one-click elements than the old one—but of course, the proof will be in whether more people buy it with the new blurb.

CHAPTER 18

EXAMPLE: DARK POLITICAL FANTASY

The following blurb describes dark political fantasy *From the Ashes*, by Kristina Gruell.

ORIGINAL BLURB

Lenathaina Morthan is the third heir of a dying line. Her Uncle, the King, has only two legitimate children. His oldest son and heir is unbalanced and sadistic and his younger son is only a child. The King is determined to use her as a bargaining chip to seal a treaty for aide with his longtime ally against the zealous Hathorite nation, which is ruled by a goddess only known as the Mystic.

The Lithonian court has many factions, some poised to help Lenathaina save the throne and the people she loves, and others ready to take advantage of the chaos to seize power. The Morthan House is on the verge of collapse and their ancient enemy, the Hathorites, is poised to move on the fractured country as soon as it does.

Can Lenathaina do her duty to her country and marry a man she has never seen to secure the alliance? When her Uncle dies, can she help the country she loves survive the fallout? If the Hathorites manage to seize power.... Her people may face a fate worse than death.

ONE-CLICK LIST

- Dark political fantasy (genre)
- Magic/mages
- Princess main character
- Impending civil war
- Forced marriage
- Mad goddess
- Spies/paranoid atmosphere

NEW BLURB

If the last princess of Morthan cannot stave off civil war, then a mad goddess will surely take the throne.

The King of Lithonia is dying. When he is gone, Lithonia will be ruled by either a cruel sadist or a six-year-old boy. Princess Lenathaina Morthan is third in line... and she has no intention of letting her country burn.

When the mad goddess of Hathor sets her gaze upon Lithonia's throne, however, the king decides to use Princess Lenathaina as a bargaining chip with his closest allies in Caeldenon. Now stranded in a foreign country, away from her center of political power, Lenathaina must use every tool at her command to scrape together allies and save her country from a fate worse than death. But will her would-be husband be one of those allies... or just another enemy?

Author Kristina Gruell debuts with a dark, high-stakes political fantasy, where every new face hides a potential threat. Pick up *From the Ashes*, and discover the shadow games that will determine the future of several nations.

EXPLANATION OF EDITS

From the Ashes originally had a cover that heavily suggested young adult fantasy. Kristina is now working on a few changes to the font and some of the decoration in order to make it look more like the dark political fantasy it really is. I did ask, at first, whether the book could squeak by as a young adult novel so that she wouldn't *need* to redo the covers—but

Kristina assured me that the book was *very* grim, and not at all meant for younger readers. After some back-and-forth chatting, it seemed clear that this was meant to be a dark political fantasy.

Once we sorted out the cover mismatch, we threw together a list of the most important one-click items, above. The original blurb didn't have a lead line—so we added one! The new lead line implies the genre with "last princess", "civil war", and "mad goddess", all of which we took from the one-click list. I thought for a while about whether I could fit in a mention of magic as well, but in the end, I figured that "mad goddess" conveyed the fantasy aspect well enough.

The new first paragraph covers a lot of the same ground as the old one, but it sums everything up both more dramatically and more succinctly. The first paragraph covers the stakes (the king is dying, his successors are awful, and bad things will happen if they take over), the main character and her starting position, and an admirable quality about her (Lenathaina cares what happens to her country, and she's determined to protect it from disaster).

The second paragraph throws a curve ball: Lenathaina might want to save her country, but she's just been bargained away to a foreign nation, and she's forced to start from scratch. Her new husband could be either an ally or an enemy, which lends itself to an interesting central conflict, and an ultimate implied question: will he help her or hinder her, as she tries to save her country?

The sales paragraph is new, and we use it to clearly state the genre so that there's no chance of confusion: this is a dark political fantasy. Kristina mentioned that some of her villains use false faces, so we've also added a hint of that, as a nod to the paranoid atmosphere. The call to action explicitly reminds the reader that they can buy the book, even while it describes the thematic feel that the reader should get from reading it.

CHAPTER 19
LAST WORD

A lot of authors tell me that writing blurbs is their least favourite part of publishing a book. I completely understand this agony, since I used to feel it myself—but more and more, I find that I enjoy writing blurbs, and I know that part of the reason for that is because I now have a concise, step-by-step process to consult whenever I write them.

I hope this process will make your own blurb-writing easier and more enjoyable.

Special thanks to Liza Street, Elsie Winters, and Kristina Gruell for giving permission to reprint their blurbs in this book. I know how tempting it can be to hide the old stuff under the carpet—but I know that plenty of other authors will be grateful for your generosity.

CHAPTER 20
EVERGREEN BLURB TEMPLATE

A lead line that conveys the genre and includes the top 3 one-click items.

An engaging hook that pulls in the reader. An introduction to the main character, and a mention of something interesting about them. Establish the stakes of the main problem.

A development in the main problem. Another potential character introduction. More one-click items. An explicit or implied question around which the story will centre.

Comparison authors and titles. Author name, title name, and genre of this book. Any important author credentials. A few snatches of the book's atmosphere. An explicit call to action to buy the book.

ABOUT THE AUTHOR

Olivia Atwater writes whimsical historical fantasy with a hint of satire. She lives in Montreal, Quebec with her fantastic, prose-inspiring husband and her two cats. When she told her second-grade history teacher that she wanted to work with history someday, she is fairly certain this isn't what either party had in mind. She has been, at various times, a historical re-enactor, a professional witch at a metaphysical supply store, a web developer, and a vending machine repairperson.

I send out writing updates and neat historical facts in the Atwater Scandal Sheets. Subscribers also get early access to chapters from each book, before anyone else!

https://oliviaatwater.com
info@oliviaatwater.com

ALSO BY OLIVIA ATWATER

REGENCY FAERIE TALES

Half a Soul

Ten Thousand Stitches

Longshadow

TALES OF THE IRON ROSE

Echoes of the Imperium (Forthcoming — 2022)

NONFICTION

Better Blurb Writing for Authors

www.ingramcontent.com/pod-product-compliance
Lightning Source LLC
Chambersburg PA
CBHW062147100526
44589CB00014B/1719